Saturnine

RHIANNON WILLIAMS

SATURNINE/ SATURNALIA

 Goggles

EYEWEAR PAMPHLET SERIES 2018

First published in 2018
by Eyewear Publishing Ltd
Suite 333, 19-21 Crawford Street
Marylebone, London W1H 1PJ
United Kingdom

Typeset with graphic design by Edwin Smet
Author photo by Ronnie Chou
Printed in England by Lightning Source

ISBN 978-1-912477-47-0

WWW.EYEWEARPUBLISHING.COM

For my mum and dad

TABLE OF CONTENTS

Goggles

MEETING SOMEBODY FOR DINNER

I walked a narrow line
demure, and used my words
as if he might hunger for them.
But the cork was pulled from the bottle and again
they gave him the wine to taste; I watched,
glad at least for words, and that the order in which they spill out
might yet possess our dining bodies,

sat in delicate balance, either side of a candle.
And I think about my tight dress, all the tightness of confirmation,
and of the dark placebo on my lips –
of what I drew on the bathroom wall with the lipstick, hidden.
Some sad, wild-eyed signifier amongst girls re-applying,
peeling feet from heels in pitiful emergencies.
And when he laid me down at last to kiss my skin
in the laboratorial closeness I allowed myself to pretend I was him.

RISEN // Μνημόσινο

Is it worth it, this August, to get up and go again?
The women's shoulders have turned to smooth brown pebbles,
but this is St Lazarus' church and you must cover them up
or suffer the stare of your neighbour, shot along the worn-wood horizon.
Warping a thin, dark yellow candle, breathing in the animal smell
of its origins and trying to will some significance into this service,
I'm waiting for the priest to say my grandmother's name –
I always miss it, his fast chant cheats me and keeps her where the dead belong.
In the afternoon, my uncles play cards while the women stand wrist-deep in offal.
They strip and drain clammy poultry, gouge out tough little hearts of vermillion,
ropy red webbing to peel and divide from the breasts and the thighs.
They roll up their sleeves and deliver. My mother eats the heart and liver.
The men take their coffee *sketo*, black-pudding-dark.
I take through a tray of tiny white cups and saucers
ceremonial under eyes sliding up from hearts and spades.
I hope they remember how she fed them; some of them she raised.
It seems to me sometimes that the service comes too late.

We were told not to enter the church while menstrual.
I did as my grandmother would have, and showed up.
She said a slap would shock blood flow to a stop.
She drank them under the table, and poured enough for everybody,
she tore up all the red roses in her garden, because it made me laugh.

A HAG-STONE

I gave the name to you, I told you
what you've picked up is a hag-stone.
Smooth and beige like the tiles miles under
beneath us, beneath Islington
beneath the hospital where I was born
under Marx and Douglas Adams
and further in with thicker ivy
the myriad of women all named Mary.

I thought you'd give it to me then,
a ceremonial swap for the name, and my day,
to turn cemetery kisses to a stone in my palm.
To pass my finger through the hole.

When you deny me something
I know you're keeping it for your girlfriend.
I wonder if she feels the same way as I do.
I don't mind certain types of sharing,
but you took her to the same place that I took you;
you're stealing ideas from me to look good. I may as well
date her myself.
Maybe I am. Maybe half of your words are hers,
the half that make me linger.

It goes into your pocket,
it will get a polish.
You will give it to her later, and wisely say
'This is a hag-stone.'

THE QUARRY

We went down to the quarry
bored with routine wearing furrows, with the air hanging between flies,
of afternoons.
We'd been told to keep an eye out, even for the things that don't look dangerous
but we became curious on the edge and the earth seemed to shift its grains
beneath our clean soles of rubber. It gave way and we dribbled into the pit in jerks
as a drop crawls down the glass. And a thorn from a dead branch tunnelled into the
membrane between my two fingers. But they were all laughing, and
so I laughed too.
The sun was lingering like it knew, like it was playing for time,
getaway-car hovering, to chivvy me home.
But it lit up the rocks in a great bovine sculpture, each lump awarded a
military stripe,
like they'd finally burst beneath the afternoon's tension and were silvery
yellow inside.
We circled it as though at a crash-landing site
under the souring sky.
One of us lifted the nearest rock, so when the sudden fox tried to slink by unseen,
he had something in his arms to hurl and he did, a knee-jerk
slaughter. Perhaps he thought it would move faster. But there it lay, a fur smear,
and I think he tried to blame it on this incubator-town, on miles of dirt and
on stagnation,
and summer boredom, and reflexes.
And if you've ever seen blood on fur, vulpine eyes gone soulless,
networks, webbing,
ed slack from wounds,
dark syrup coalescing,
you'll know how I felt walking home.

IF IN A SEA BIG ENOUGH

Alighting at King's Cross
I think of planetary foils to keep me calm.
Huge space-wakes, black and oily
imagined foils like solid air, or some
deep sea see-through creature barely there.
The measured, joyous ploughing of the planets,
unearthing the solid Roman silver
of a moon and onwards rolling slowly
like a tongued boiled sweet, like a laugh,
bigger than obscenity,
a briefcase smug on a matted tube seat,
or that man on the Victoria line, calling
a stranger a cunt at barely 9am:
the planets turn their cratered cheeks.
Saturn is tilted towards us this season,
making it easier for us to see.
I'd scale myself up to be my totem
if I could, to hold everyone close
because if in a sea big enough, I'd float.

Goggles

HESMOVEDON

The worst has come true;
I can do the forbidden now.
Unpick my jinxes frantic as I
come undone like a hope
not knotted tight enough.
It's the end of the world
and the heat of the apocalypse
bleeds and draws me, blinds me
through my own eyelids greedily,
the bolshy white of disbelief
filtered red and mock-tender, you ok?
As the curvature recedes
like a smirk
like a bubble bursting
documentary-slow.
Rainbows turn to skins
just flesh, in the end
after all.

CHIROKITIA

I used a powerful torch one night,
and painted myself onto the side of the opposite mountain.
Our town's small enough to frustrate; small enough to walk out on,
so we'd gone walking, and set up camp beside an old scorch.
Paths of earth trodden hard and erased of grass
showed us how people navigate dry evergreens,
passive in the breeze, and a floor of sun-brittle needles and leaves.
We sat down without a sheet, the ground humming back
midday's heat. The mountains became navy knuckles,
and the Milky Way lazed above like a dusty streak on a stray dog.
We stared till the scrambled silver became more familiar,
and charted wings, a word, a face. Soon it was us
the sky took orders from, us standing and facing the stars
like children stirring embers to ashes with a stick.
When we'd kicked out the fire after dinner, a city had spread out:
we were governing ghosts above its lights, their lines
distant and gold as the dots on deep-sea fish.
Then I'd loved our island for how it softens beneath our feet
and keeps our traces, as though it finds them precious.

SUBMISSION

I told myself I would
plate up my heart blue
if it would snag him.
The freezing thrill
of going under, dunked
and being covered by the love.
Too dark to see
my insecurities.
A love like deep sea pressure,
the gas giant pull.
I would ring my shattered moonlets
into a torque for him
and this way I would float,
twined. A serpent doting. Round his spine.
Until that darkest time of night
when my outline disappears.
It is too dark to see my fears
and there is a pull stronger than his.
Sneaking out the
way a woman learns,
I sneak out of myself
and fill the sea whole.

MEMORIAL

I am told not to cross my legs in church
as you were told not to meet the eyes of the boys you passed
in the village, treading carefully, searching on the ground
for the crisp grenades of pine cones to collect and sell.
You didn't choose to sew and starch, develop factory fingers,
that they would cease to belong to you.
Your name is taken, given to a new baby sister, and you carry on
carrying your mother's babies and you carry on caring.
And now you must marry a man you have never shared a room with
and have babies of your own, scrape savings to send back home.
Work lies around the house in folded piles, and waiting in the kitchen.

And you'd never know it from this photo where
hand to your chest
you are helpless with mirth at how your sixty candles
have heaved themselves back into life and light once again, because
when would you ever have learned
what happens when magnesium burns?

Now the incense curls. A grey area.
From his fingers swings a golden carriage for you
arriving much too late I think.
And when I stab that candle into the sand
it is not your death but your life
I atone
I stab.

OVERWHELM

I'm hurting just organising this,
brainstorming places for us to visit.
You and I can't ever take a walk alone again.
We will always be hand-in-hand-in-hand
with the memory of our old relationship.
It tugs us towards old haunts we'd rather skip
and not taste a transportive beer
regress some years.
Food and drink and sun make a sleek skin
to gild a life with all the negatives discarded.
Sometimes it's worth taking a short-cut
using the vacuum of the tube to evade
the city's sensory Russian roulette.
I don't often wish for oblivion
but when I'm brimming with hot tears
just from the kebab smells of Tottenham
it feels like the right prescription.

RAINBOW TROUT

The city was dull before
we applied our flame.
The milky Thames
is the stripe on a rainbow trout
and wobbly streets
burrows of time
soaked in old purple wine.
Between us, a length of twine.
If I move, your muscles follow.
If you move, so do mine.

My friend's older brother caught a fish.
A fat one; its compact body convulsing,
the O of its mouth not surprised, only blind.
The trout-jerk is how I felt
each time I could not look away.
Each time I thought I had to stay.
Or uncovered my eyes too soon –
panic is the flicker-thud of fish meat
slapping the decking, leaking salty life.

We are leaving the city now, you know.
The same place we grew up dying for a bite of.
Our lot are leaving, and writing articles
about fresh air and leaving the meanness behind.
As though we don't still share the sky,
and all the rivers are matching ribbons.

I forget the city makes us cruel. But let's not leave.
When I find myself struggling
will you unhook the words from my mouth,
take them out?

THIEVING

They told me I was not allowed
to take anything back to the other side.
It didn't seem like a site of cruelty,
a place of bad memories. Piles of stone
and an old wooden chair outside, left with
a froth of curling wicker tongues.
The air felt soft, like leaf mould.
The four walls of my grandmother's shack,
propping each other up like old women
who remembered too much, begged me
to promise I'd be back for them another day.
A thin chicken pecked a dead-plant lattice,
the flat, trampled foil of age, or of heavy boots –
'There,' said mum, 'is where she used to
hang the radio from the tree, while she sewed.'
And into the pockets of my shorts I snuck
a rock, a small pine cone, the fuzzy cat's-ear
of an almond's outer shell, a piece of straw.
I sweated through border control,
thumbs stroking the pieces of land I'd reclaimed.

RECURRING THOUGHT I

is about Dan Bilzerian throwing a porn actress into his pool
from his roof; the bone in her foot cracking off the poolside tiles
is a final straw.
Is about why we are cool with this; is about why he expects us to be
is it because this is another type of bodily rental
is it because this is another trick to turn, and she has chosen to splay
and so this is where she stays, in the cyan, splayed.
Still, sometimes it feels like I've seen many a man
like Dan
up there, splayed
all steaming existence
all mansion-top colossus
and he looks I think, beard neat, legs thick, packed with red affirmation,
all poster paint red in the setting sun
like a home-made flag on a fort
(poor, bare, forked animal)
I think about his bones and his sinews and his blood and his ligaments;
about outer space rolling them between her finger and thumb
and flicking them back to earth.

THE BEAST

I have seen the poster girls and boys of depression
on Netflix;
they are beautiful and relatable
arrangements of limbs on-screen.

A languidity; a lily petal girl bruised by mystery.
These lips have never borne
the deliberate salivating of the beast, brought up one night
out of the blue; out of the raw throat
as it claws at her arms trying to make itself a breathing hole.
The shame as bright as a tulip
in knowing you have left the spit on your chin
for your parents to wipe.

The beast can drive, and was the driver
when you woke up somewhere new, and the world felt different.
And you began to think too much,
unable to see yourself without the fingerprints of the world.
Of all the people you wish you had the energy to help.
You are stained with rage, and the beast sits
on the hospital bed of your body like a hag
invisible to your family.

The beast bites out a hole in the skin of the world
and through it you can see too much.
Like outer space, it's an emptiness, and a full mouth,
both a silence, and the thing that has been caught in the silence,
fingers in the workings.
Eyes static as jammed moons, and cheeks crammed with terrible secrets.

SURROUNDED

6.5 million square feet of Miami-pink floats in Biscayne Bay,
puddling the islands: they look like they've been trodden into bubblegum.
The stuff ripples like a tropical flatworm, like my skirt floating up around me
when I wade out waist deep, to see how far I can go. The fabric gets heavy,
the islands are surrounded, the fur of each tree a mould spore on pink buttercream.
It looks light as silk. Though wet cloth is weighty, I imagine it keeps us afloat.
I always find the same faces in town, piggybank pink; they stud the strip
like shells you find embedded in the shore. I try to count them from where I lean
on the warm, paint-flaking metal of the balustrade. But they all look the same.
And when the pink flesh and peel fall away here they'll stay on the dormant stone.
On a dot, in a spatter on the planet, petals not pink, but brown, wet, and stuck.

HALLOWED HOME

A topography
of solid air
and
the birdshit
in translucent stains
wet petals on the pews
clambered over
to reach his mugs
cave-painted, his blanket, his
spare pair of shoes.

And a lump
(a pillow is it?)
but I won't, can't lift the dust sheet back.
(The space between the objects
hisses *bedroom*, if I
touch a thing
the veneer of territory cracks.)

I'm being selfish,
whispered words, that lift
a hymn sheet, ruffle feathers
as he asks, why not just cut
the whole place up? And give

the folk a home.
A jewel in leaflogged Haggerston,
winking from the gutter.

Wiped clean, now warm,
this church the gift of winter's fire.

And fire won't stay quiet –
and neither will the attic space
on Monday nights, when from the strings
he wrings out notes
to change the function of the air.

BREAKING THE BAG

I dreamed I was pregnant again. Not of the swelling,
just of the fear. Fear like iron, heavy and rusty.
A pressing decision. We had been talking about abortion law
in distant Arkansas: a law that needed the father's consent.
The sky was sliding through its pastel spectrum
still, there was some heat. And for once we'd disagreed
and I'd remembered what a woman is, even here, even now.

What seemed to snag was the mistake
and that it must be paid for. (By woman and man, I am told.
Still, I think of stretching, swelling, draining, tearing,
I think of how children need to be wanted.)
In this moment my dream-baby's made a litmus for morality,
a measure of my womanhood and what I choose to do with it.
No, I haven't spent my life in training, I want to say
and I am not ready, and I am afraid –
why is it these debates become like wading through a dream
where my mouth opens but cannot speak.
Even now, at your verdict on my body, I can't help but hope to please:
it's that woman's wiring I swear
I'll take the steps to cut and switch someday.

And the women I love and the women I speak to are heavy with desire.
The desire to work, and move, unmarked,
to speak and dress without commentary, and to cut out their hearts.
To keep them in small boxes, and use them privately, in the dark.
I want to lie down in the thick cold grass,
I wish I could close like the roses at night.
But what a woman seems to be is free as far as being a woman allows.
It allows us to live on a beam. To live without breaking the bag.
I think we can have our fill until we slip

and then we carry our penance to term.
Punishment's a mirror held up to a woman.
Punishment's just another female bodily function.
The pain speaks of mortality, and when it
shivers through my body and pulls sharp like a drawstring
I feel it's as possessive of me as a lover.
And he has never had his body possessed by another.

But it is words that frighten me,
and if his word decides where I am for a lifetime
or my next nine months: then we know what a woman is.
And I don't want to be one.

When it comes, I will hold my love tight like an emerald
til it digs in and hurts, when I choose to hurt and when I choose to bleed,
only then will I sit still. I want the streets to part for me
and the words will shrink and run like mercury.
And love will come deliberately.
No, the place the arrow shoots from
is the last thing I would want to be.

SAKURA EMOJI

May is doubtless pink, and whether
this is down to synesthesia
or blossom inspiration, I don't know.
May's a moodboard, May's a new start, only
I have never liked the phrase 'girl power'
and when I saw the woman at the station
with the tattoo between her 2 tanned shoulders
look like a girl act like a lady think like a man
I thought how clever they are to make us despise ourselves.

At the crest, May rolls over porcine shy of a gutting.
You thought you were ready, you thought
you'd beaten all the other girls.
Against blue, May will never not be pink.

APHRODITE'S ROCK

You won't find the apple core or dented can
of cartoon trash. The froth of rocks is kept clean,
this bay a white slice of a smile for the island.
Wedding couples are photographed up here
against the terrifying blue. Tiny on their biggest day.
Just off the motorway is where Aphrodite was born,
you can park your car here and see the rocks,
the foam that names her caught between them,
blue muscle and arterial purple
sculpting the white rock into scoops and points.
People cluster on a cliff edge to photograph her rock.
It languishes there at the pointer of the spit,
a huge tilted breast of baked mud.
We forget that we were once underwater
and overwrite the inscriptions of the sea
with lovehearts scored deep into soft chalky rock,
the lodged fish spines of Greek capital letters.
You can imagine her rising groggy and heavy,
dragging herself up: so vast a tide peeling from her dark hip
would submerge the island once again.

RIHANNA AS JUDITH

For Summer I keep my hair waist length
like Rihanna when she had those cherry waves.
Mine are not as glossy but I like the feel of them
and I'm trying to unlearn the act of keeping things to myself
like my opinions. In the summer they melt and run
a bit much. I listen to the radio more in the Summer too,
in the garden, hibiscus-red and baked-sky blue,
to remind me of her flowing through the town
drinking coconut milk and dancing with the men.
'Maybe she likes it rough' said a boy in my class
of the Indian girl killed by her attackers.
I think about the songs sung by the women I know
about the girl whose jaw he broke to stop her struggling
still, he coulda been somebody's son

anyway what was I saying about Summer
I guess what I want to know
as I play with the sunbleached radio, is
why the subject of the most popular and commercially successful song
about rape
is the guilt of the victim for killing her rapist?

I'm glad I shot the bastard
shot the bastard
shot the bastard

man down

SNAPDRAGON

In the bathroom they were discussing you loudly,
a few girls down, along our reflected frieze.
Pretending there was something in my eye
I marvelled at their slim, candle limbs without thinking.
The way we wish that we could be each other,
the way we marvel at the cleverness of nature.
Chin halo-lit by a buttercup, still
we worm our fingers into lady's slippers for the pleasure,
and giggle, gape, at neat clitoria, orchid,
the papery skull of the snapdragon's pod
like we made up sex and death all by ourselves,
and nature plagiarised.
And then we wonder, what she's trying to say with
that bold lip, this little crimp?
They were saying you like blondes
and despite myself, I cursed.

I am not the snap of the snapdragon
but I will try for you its colour,
and be the yellow from the room at
John Soane's where, all saluting
with their Dulux pads, they flip to find a match
but a candle can't be held.
I do imagine in time the flame will burn bluer,
shrug the lemon cream frills slowly down past its shoulders
and bend before the eyes and prayers.
And if I'd bend,
curl like a fortune fish in your palm,
soft and unprogrammable as wax,
still over your warm shoulder I'd see in the wall
through to the crippled plumbing of a woman, trapped.

Goggles

KALOPANAYIOTIS

At the back of the monastery are the solid prayers of waxworks
made by those who can't use priesthood or paint.
Models of single injured limbs lean on the wall like liquorice sticks,
parts sat in rows like wares, knobbled fingers and supple noses,
the uneven mounds of two breasts, a head.
Effigies of whole babies in ochre wax lie mollusc-like
on the flagstones. I breathe in their musky fatty smell
and wonder if wax magic works, and can heal.
A huge Saint Mary dominates, the paint carob dark and primitive,
her shrouded curve familiar. She looks older and sadder,
her eyes almond-shaped and underscored. I might admit
that she scares me more than the crude ancient saints
surrounding us, the dark threat of their paint coating the walls.
Some have white, scribbled voids instead of eyes,
scars from the island's invasion: a sharp-tooled overwriting.
Still, the islanders bring their wax before blind saints,
in the hope that wounds can smooth over and seal.

BURIAL

This is not the walk we took as teenagers;
the sand has shifted and exchanged its grains so many times since then.
But like an animal I see our old trail glow, and take it for security.
Alone, through the dark blue sand, cold and ashy,
its shells and trysts, traced names and turtle eggs
submerged, preserved in a deep-beach archive.
The top layer a fine, crumbled mothwing
churned by the nonplussed nightwalkers of 2017.

Goggles

SWAN

Things are different now, or they're meant to be.
There is a kind of lazy understanding that we all accept each other,
so it felt alien, one night, when someone questioned the adamant
femininity of your clothes.
Drunk, but still those eyes they held your flesh in place expectantly
to see what you would do next. Your long white neck
turned a little, and the certainty of your nose considered the dark beyond
the balcony bars
and in your eyes, darkly outlined, I saw reflected the cruelty of children.

Two boys shot down a swan, a bone china embellishment claimed
from the centre of a pond.
It was a long and empty summer afternoon,
they had been torturing a third, silent boy; they sent him to gather the
warm white bundle; darkly leaking
the proud origami crumpled.
And they snapped and carved its frothing wings from its deadness
they bound them hard to the boy's skinny arms
to see what he would do next. For a moment,
the blood moved like a slow contemplation, like it was inching through
crystals of snow.
And then he beat the air before his attackers, tore himself free,
a gore-dripping bird,
and flew away.

THANKS/CREDITS

Thank you to my family and their incredible capacity for patience and love; to Todd, Alex and Edwin at Eyewear for their invaluable help; to Feminist Internet, who have been more of a source of courage and inspiration than they know, and to the doorman at The Old Firehouse in Exeter who let me in for free one night, on the condition that I credit him in my first piece of published work.